THE WORLD'S
GREATEST COLLECTION OF
DAFFY DEFINITIONS

You'll never be
at a loss for words again!

In this "mini-dictionary" of over 500 daffy definitions covering every letter of the alphabet, bestselling humorist Bob Phillips gives you clever, silly, and thought-provoking vocabulary stretchers that will spark your conversations and increase your poise.

The World's Greatest Collection of Daffy Definitions is great for:

- spicing up family times
- livening up your workplace
- newsletter or bulletin "fillers"
- entertaining friends
- salvaging the time when stuck in a waiting room or a long line

The perfect way to ensure you'll always have the "last word" that leaves your audience speechless!

For a double-dose of laughs, turn the book over and try your hand at *The World's Greatest Collection of Riddles* on the reverse side.

About the Author

With over a dozen joke books, game books, and books of colorful wisdom to his credit, BOB PHILLIPS is a master compiler of the light and humorous side of life.

When Bob isn't out scouring the earth for humor, he directs Hume Lake Camps, one of America's largest youth camping programs, and serves as a licensed marriage, family, and child counselor.

THE WORLD'S GREATEST COLLECTION OF RIDDLES

With his special knack for seeing the humorous and the unusual side of everyday life, Bob Phillips introduces an assortment of over 400 zany riddles to keep you smiling and guessing.

For a refreshing change in your day, take a "riddle break" through topics ranging from:

- time
- food
- money
- love
- occupations

- history
- animals
- geometry
- spelling
- children

*Guaranteed to bring a smile
and a new perspective on life!*

Share your favorites from *The World's Greatest Collection of Riddles* with family and friends to brighten their day with a chuckle.

For a double-bonus of humor, turn the book over and enjoy *The World's Greatest Collection of Daffy Definitions*—over 500 crazy "one-liners" in mini-dictionary format.

About the Author

With over a dozen joke books, game books, and books of colorful wisdom to his credit, BOB PHILLIPS is a master compiler of the light and humorous side of life.

When Bob isn't out scouring the earth for humor, he directs Hume Lake Camps, one of America's largest youth camping programs, and serves as a licensed marriage, family, and child counselor.

WORLD'S GREATEST COLLECTION OF

OF

Riddles

Compiled by BOB PHILLIPS

HARVEST HOUSE PUBLISHERS
Eugene, Oregon 97402

**THE WORLD'S
GREATEST COLLECTION OF
RIDDLES**

Phillips, Bob, 1940-
    The world's greatest collection of daffy definitions;
The world's greatest collection of riddles.

    No collective t.p. Titles transcribed from individual
title pages.
    1. Riddles, Juvenile.   2. Riddles.   I. Phillips,
Bob, 1940- . World's greatest collection of riddles. 1989.
II. Title: World's greatest collection of daffy definitions.
III. Title: World's greatest collection of riddles.
PN6371.5.P49   1989   818'.5402   88-32811
ISBN 0-89081-700-6

Q: What is it that has a heart in its head?
A: Lettuce.

* * *

Q: What do they call the friendship that one movie actor has for another?
A: Jealousy

* * *

Q: If there is a red house on the right and a blue house on the left, where is the White House?
A: In Washington, D. C.

* * *

Q: Why did the jelly roll?
A: Because it saw the apple turnover.

Q: Why is it dangerous for farmers to plant peas during a war?

A: The enemy might come along and shell them.

* * *

Q: How do you make a slow employee fast?

A: Don't give him anything to eat for a while.

* * *

Q: If you were invited out to dinner and on sitting down saw nothing but a beet, what would you say?

A: "That beet's all!"

* * *

Q: What do they call a collector of old magazines?

A: A doctor.

* * *

Q: What are the largest ants in the world?

A: Elephants.

* * *

Q: Why shouldn't American girls learn Russian?

A: Because one tongue is enough for any girl.

Q: What kind of dress do you have but never wear?
A: Your address.

*   *   *

Q: What are 365 periods of disappointment called?
A: A year.

*   *   *

Q: What should you do if you feel strongly about graffiti?
A: Sign a partition.

*   *   *

Q: When do you put a mouse in your sister's bed?
A: When you can't find a frog.

*   *   *

Q: What do you call a pig that took an airplane ride?
A: Swine flu.

*   *   *

Q: Why does the Statue of Liberty stand in New York Harbor?
A: Because it can't sit down.

Q: Where do fish keep their life savings?
A: In a riverbank.

*　　*　　*

Q: What sort of offspring does a stupid florist have?
A: Blooming idiots.

*　　*　　*

Q: If a soft answer turneth away wrath, what does a hard answer do for you?
A: It turneth wrath your way.

*　　*　　*

Q: What gets lost every time you stand up?
A: Your lap.

*　　*　　*

Q: How should you greet a German barber?
A: "Herr Dresser."

*　　*　　*

Q: What kind of waiter never accepts tips?
A: A dumb waiter.

Q: How would you define the daffodil?

A: A goofy pickle.

* * *

Q: Why would a compliment from a chicken be an insult?

A: Because it's a fowl remark.

* * *

Q: What did the grape say when it was stepped on by an elephant?

A: Nothing...it just gave a little wine.

* * *

Q: What is the difference between a mouse and a young lady?

A: One harms the cheese, and the other charms the he's.

* * *

Q: What can overpower a karate master without hurting him?

A: Sleep.

Q: What kind of sentence would you get if you broke the law of gravity?

A: A suspended one.

* * *

Q: Why is an ex-boxer like a beehive?

A: An ex-boxer is an ex-pounder; an expounder is a commentator; a common tater is an Irish tater; an Irish tater is a speck'd tater; a spectator is a beholder; and a bee-holder is a beehive.

* * *

Q: What did Snow White say when her pictures did not arrive back from the photo service?

A: Someday my prints will come.

* * *

Q: Why isn't your ear 12 inches long?

A: If it were, it would be a foot.

* * *

Q: What does not break, no matter how far it falls?

A: A leaf.

* * *

Q: What is the best weather for gathering hay?

A: When it rains pitchforks.

Q: What do you do with a blue monster?
A: Cheer him up.

* * *

Q: Why does a dog wag its tail?
A: Because it wants to.

* * *

Q: What country makes you shiver with cold?
A: Chile.

* * *

Q: How long can a goose stand on one leg?
A: Try it and see.

* * *

Q: How do you spell mousetrap in three letters?
A: C-A-T.

* * *

Q: Why does a little boy look one way and then the other way before crossing the street?
A: Because he can't look both ways at the same time.

Q: What word is always pronounced wrong?
A: Wrong.

* * *

Q: Why did the simpleton always handle money with his toes?
A: So it wouldn't slip through his fingers.

* * *

Q: What fish is man's best friend?
A: The dogfish.

* * *

Q: When do hens change their sex?
A: At night—when they are roosters.

* * *

Q: Why do we all go to bed?
A: Because the bed will not come to us.

* * *

Q: What increases in value by half when you turn it upside down?
A: The number 6.

Q: What kind of seafood makes a good sandwich?
A: Jellyfish.

* * *

Q: What can you make by putting two banana peels together?
A: A pair of slippers.

* * *

Q: What pen is never used for writing?
A: A pigpen.

* * *

Q: Which is faster—hot or cold?
A: Hot's faster. You can catch cold.

* * *

Q: What do they call someone whose opinion differs from their own?
A: A radical.

* * *

Q: Why is a kiss like gossip?
A: Because it goes from mouth to mouth.

Q: What cord is full of knots which no one can untie?

A: A cord of wood.

* * *

Q: What did Columbus first stand on when he discovered America?

A: His feet.

* * *

Q: What do they call cabs lined up at the Dallas airport?

A: The yellow rows of taxis.

* * *

Q: What has four wheels, two horns, gives milk, and eats grass?

A: A cow on a skateboard.

* * *

Q: What has four legs and only one foot?

A: A bed.

* * *

Q: In what month do girls talk the least?

A: February—because it is the shortest.

Q: Why do birds fly south for the winter?
A: Because it's too far to walk.

* * *

Q: What would a home be without children?
A: Quiet.

* * *

Q: Which is correct: The yolk of an egg IS white?
   Or the yolks of eggs ARE white?
A: Neither, the yolk of an egg is yellow.

* * *

Q: What lives in the forest, puts out fires, and has
   eight arms?
A: Smokey the Octopus.

* * *

Q: How can a leopard change his spots?
A: By moving.

* * *

Q: How do sailors identify Long Island?
A: By the Sound.

Q: What question can never be answered by saying "Yes"?

A: Are you asleep?

* * *

Q: When the clock strikes 13, what time is it?

A: Time to get the clock fixed.

* * *

Q: What kind of lights did Noah have on his Ark?

A: Floodlights.

* * *

Q: Which is heavier, a half moon or a full moon?

A: A half moon, because the full moon is lighter.

* * *

Q: What is the surest way to keep water from coming into your house?

A: Don't pay your water bill.

* * *

Q: How did the father flea get home for Christmas?

A: By Greyhound.

Q: What's round and dangerous?

A: A vicious circle.

* * *

Q: What is a bore?

A: A person who can change the topic of a conversation faster than you can change it back to yours.

* * *

Q: What is another name for income tax?

A: Capital punishment.

* * *

Q: What would you call a gold digger?

A: A human gimmee pig.

* * *

Q: What do they call six women with one luncheon check?

A: Chaos.

* * *

Q: What do they call a man who knows a good joke when he steals one?

A: A writer of riddle books.

Q: What did Mrs. Bullet say to Mr. Bullet?

A: "Darling, I'm going to have a BB!"

* * *

Q: What did the 300-pound mouse say?

A: Here kitty, kitty, kitty.

* * *

Q: What do they call a boxer who gets beat up in a fight?

A: A sore loser.

* * *

Q: What is another name for a nightclub?

A: A rolling pin.

* * *

Q: How do you make a Big Mac monster burger?

A: You put two people patties, special sauce, lettuce, cheese, pickles, and onions on a sesame seed bun.

* * *

Q: Why does a fireman wear red suspenders?

A: To hold up his pants.

Q: What falls often but never gets hurt?
A: Rain.

*   *   *

Q: How should you refer to a tailor when you don't remember his name?
A: As Mr. So-and-So.

*   *   *

Q: Name a very rude bird.
A: A mockingbird.

*   *   *

Q: What is another name for coffee?
A: Break fluid.

*   *   *

Q: What was the largest island before Australia was discovered?
A: Australia.

*   *   *

Q: Where can you always find happiness?
A: In the dictionary.

Q: When is it proper to refer to a person as a pig?
A: When he is a boar.

*   *   *

Q: What is always behind time?
A: The back of a watch.

*   *   *

Q: Which day is stronger—Sunday or Monday?
A: Sunday is stronger. Monday is a weekday.

*   *   *

Q: How many balls of string would it take to reach to the moon?
A: One, if it was long enough.

*   *   *

Q: Which is the largest room in the world?
A: The room for improvement.

*   *   *

Q: Where do Eskimos keep their money?
A: In a snowbank.

Q: What did the nearsighted Gingerbread Boy use for eyes?

A: Contact raisins.

* * *

Q: What do you do if you have cobwebs in your brain?

A: Use a vacuum cleaner.

* * *

Q: What do you call a nut that never remembers?

A: A forget-me-nut.

* * *

Q: What's green and goes slam, slam, slam, slam?

A: A four-door pickle.

* * *

Q: How do you spell Mississippi with one eye?

A: Close one eye and spell it.

* * *

Q: What is always coming but never arrives?

A: Tomorrow.

Q: Why are oysters lazy?
A: Because they are always found in beds.

* * *

Q: What did one volcano say to the other volcano?
A: I lava you.

* * *

Q: What do you call a person who's mad about chocolate?
A: A cocoa-nut.

* * *

Q: What do they call a smoking mathematician?
A: A puff adder.

* * *

Q: Why was Cleopatra so hard to get along with?
A: She was the queen of denial.

* * *

Q: What is the right kind of timber for castles in the air?
A: Sunbeams.

Q: Where is the capital of the United States?
A: All over the world.

*   *   *

Q: What happens to a lion who crosses the desert on Christmas Day?
A: He gets sandy claws.

*   *   *

Q: What do you call a sunburn on your stomach?
A: A pot roast.

*   *   *

Q: What was the elephant doing in the road?
A: About three miles an hour.

*   *   *

Q: When can you see yourself in a place you've never been?
A: When you look into a mirror.

*   *   *

Q: Where would you send a man to get an appetite?
A: To Hungary.

Q: Do you know how long cows should be milked?

A: Of course! The same as short ones.

* * *

Q: Why did Humpty-Dumpty fall off the wall?

A: To make the nursery rhyme go right.

* * *

Q: What is the best day to fry food?

A: Friday.

* * *

Q: What's the quickest way to collect on your life insurance?

A: Tell a hippo that his mother wears combat boots.

* * *

Q: What room can no one enter?

A: A mushroom.

* * *

Q: How do you become a coroner?

A: You have to take a stiff examination.

Q: What two letters got kicked out of the alphabet for being rotten?
A: D-K.

*　　*　　*

Q: How did the rocket lose his job?
A: He was fired.

*　　*　　*

Q: What keeps the moon from falling?
A: Its beams, of course.

*　　*　　*

Q: What did the judge say when the skunk came into the courtroom?
A: "Odor in the court!"

*　　*　　*

Q: What did one tail pipe say to the other tail pipe?
A: I'm exhausted.

*　　*　　*

Q: What do you say when you meet a two-headed monster?
A: "Hello, hello!"

Q: Where is the best place to have a broken bone?

A: On someone else.

* * *

Q: Why did the boy take a hammer to bed with him?

A: He wanted to hit the sack.

* * *

Q: What is purple and crazy?

A: A grape nut.

* * *

Q: What happens when a flock of geese lands in a volcano?

A: They cook their own gooses.

* * *

Q: Why are telephone rates so high in Iran?

A: Because everyone speaks Persian-to-Persian.

* * *

Q: What do you get if you cross a steer with a tadpole?

A: A bullfrog.

Q: What do you get when you cross an elephant with a computer?

A: A 5000-pound know-it-all.

* * *

Q: Why did the whale cross the road?

A: To get to the other side.

* * *

Q: What did one elevator say to the other elevator?

A: I think I'm coming down with something.

* * *

Q: What's the longest word in the dictionary?

A: Smiles. There's a mile between the first and last letter.

* * *

Q: What do you call a veterinarian with laryngitis?

A: A hoarse doctor.

* * *

Q: What becomes of most love triangles?

A: They turn into wreck-tangles.

Q: Why did the traffic light turn red?

A: If you had to change in front of all those people, you'd turn red too.

* * *

Q: Who can stay single even if he marries many women?

A: A minister.

* * *

Q: What kind of fish is the most stupid?

A: A simple salmon.

* * *

Q: What does the plumber say to his wife when she talks too much?

A: Pipe down.

* * *

Q: What word do most people like best?

A: The last.

* * *

Q: What did the sea say to the shore?

A: Nothing. It just waved.

Q: How often do big ocean liners sink?
A: Only once.

*   *   *

Q: What do you call a crazy man who lives at the mouth of the Amazon?
A: A Brazil nut.

*   *   *

Q: When is it bad luck to have a black cat follow you?
A: When you are a mouse.

*   *   *

Q: What kind of sea creature is like an expression of disbelief?
A: Abalone.

*   *   *

Q: Name a carpenter's tool you can spell forward and backward the same way.
A: Level.

*   *   *

Q: What well-known animal drives an automobile?
A: The road hog.

Q: How do you make an elephant float?
A: Put him with two scoops of ice cream in a glass of soda.

* * *

Q: How many sides does a circle have?
A: Two. Inside and outside.

* * *

Q: How does a dentist examine a crocodile's teeth?
A: Very carefully!

* * *

Q: What two opposites mean the same thing?
A: Half-full and half-empty.

* * *

Q: What is the oldest form of social security?
A: Suspenders.

* * *

Q: What do they call it when a Cub Scout washes his hands?
A: Erosion.

Q: What do they call a textbook wired for sound?
A: A professor.

* * *

Q: Why are writers the strangest creatures in the world?
A: Because their tales come out of their heads.

* * *

Q: Why is the stork associated with birth?
A: Because we all come into this world stork naked.

* * *

Q: Why is a wig like a lie?
A: Because it's a falsehood.

* * *

Q: Where does a pig go to pawn his watch?
A: He goes to a ham hock shop.

* * *

Q: How long is a Chinaman?
A: Of course! (How Long is his name.)

* * *

Q: What do we need armies for?
A: To keep our handies on.

Q: Why should people never suffer from hunger in the Sahara Desert?

A: Because of the sand which is there.

*   *   *

Q: If two is company and three is a crowd, what are four and five?

A: Nine.

*   *   *

Q: How do you divide 19 apples equally among 13 boys if 8 of the apples are small?

A: By making applesauce.

*   *   *

Q: Which is larger, Mr. Larger or Mr. Larger's baby?

A: The baby is a little Larger.

*   *   *

Q: What do you call someone who steals pigs?

A: A hamburglar.

*   *   *

Q: Why should a man never tell his secrets in a cornfield?

A: Because there are too many ears there, and they might be shocked.

Q: What do you get if you cross a skeleton with a great detective?

A: Sherlock Bones.

* * *

Q: What kind of robbery may not be dangerous?

A: A safe robbery.

* * *

Q: Who was Snow White's brother?

A: Egg White ... get the yolk?

* * *

Q: Why does electricity shock people?

A: Because it doesn't know how to conduct itself.

* * *

Q: What is the Lone Ranger's first name?

A: The.

* * *

Q: Which key is the hardest to turn?

A: A donkey.

Q: What did one horse say to the other?

A: "I can't remember your mane but your pace is familiar."

* * *

Q: What did one bowl of pudding say to the other bowl of pudding?

A: You're pudding me on.

* * *

Q: Which is the best side of the bed to sleep on?

A: The top side.

* * *

Q: What did one stuck-up person say to another?

A: Nothing.

* * *

Q: What will stay hot longest in the refrigerator?

A: Red pepper.

* * *

Q: What is the difference between the rising sun and the setting sun?

A: All the difference in the world.

Q: Who rides a dog and was a Confederate general during the Civil War?

A: Robert E. Flea.

*   *   *

Q: What is another name for a cracked pot?

A: A psycho-ceramic.

*   *   *

Q: What do you call a hotdog who always speaks his mind?

A: A frankfurter.

*   *   *

Q: What is the oldest tree?

A: The elder.

*   *   *

Q: What would a cannibal be who ate his mother's sister?

A: An aunt eater.

*   *   *

Q: What is the value of the moon?

A: Four quarters.

Q: How can you change a pumpkin into another vegetable?

A: Throw it down onto the ground and it will become squash.

* * *

Q: Why did the shrimp blush?

A: Because somebody saw it in the salad dressing.

* * *

Q: What is the difference between an elephant and a flea?

A: An elephant can have fleas, but a flea can't have elephants.

* * *

Q: What does a hen do just before she stands on one foot?

A: She lifts up the other one.

* * *

Q: What makes an empty matchbox superior to any other?

A: It is matchless.

Q: Which Chinese city is like a man looking through a keyhole?

A: Peking.

* * *

Q: What steps should you take if a tiger charges you?

A: Long ones.

* * *

Q: How far is it from one end of the earth to the other?

A: A day's journey. (The sun does it in a day.)

* * *

Q: What do they call someone who can stick to a reducing diet?

A: A good loser.

* * *

Q: What is the difference between a hungry person and a greedy person?

A: One longs to eat and the other eats too long.

* * *

Q: If your dog were eating your book, what would you do?

A: I would take the words right out of his mouth.

Q: What happened when the dog visited the flea circus?

A: He stole the show.

* * *

Q: With what two animals do you always go to bed?

A: Two calves.

* * *

Q: What's the most popular gardening magazine?

A: Weeder's Digest.

* * *

Q: What is so brittle that it can be broken just by naming it?

A: Silence.

* * *

Q: Why would you expect a fisherman to be more honest than a shepherd?

A: Because a fisherman lives by hook and a shepherd lives by crook.

* * *

Q: What is green and pecks on trees?

A: Woody Wood Pickle.

Q: When is a black dog not a black dog?
A: When he is a greyhound.

*   *   *

Q: What is the difference between a cat and a match?
A: The cat lights on its feet and the match on its head.

*   *   *

Q: When is an elevator not an elevator?
A: When it is going down.

*   *   *

Q: What happens when a chimp twists his ankle?
A: He gets a monkey wrench.

*   *   *

Q: What do you call a carpenter who lends tools to his neighbor?
A: A saw loser.

*   *   *

Q: When is it right for you to lie?
A: When you are in bed.

Q: If joy is the opposite of sorrow, what is the opposite of woe?

A: Giddyap!

* * *

Q: How can you tell a Jersey cow from any other cow?

A: By its license plate.

* * *

Q: What will change a pear into a pearl?

A: The letter L.

* * *

Q: What do you call a cow eating grass?

A: A lawn mooer.

* * *

Q: How can you be sure the engine in your car isn't missing?

A: Lift the hood and look in.

* * *

Q: If a farmer sold 500 bushels of wheat for a dollar a bushel, what would he get?

A: A lot of customers.

Q: What day of the year is a command to go forward?
A: March 4th.

* * *

Q: What kind of ears does an engine have?
A: Engineers.

* * *

Q: Who invented the grandfather clock?
A: Pendulum Franklin.

* * *

Q: What kind of saw lives in the sea?
A: A seesaw.

* * *

Q: What do you call a newborn beetle?
A: A baby buggy!

* * *

Q: What kind of timepiece does a witch wear?
A: A witchwatch.

Q: If one horse is shut up in a stable and another one is running loose down the road, which horse is singing "Don't Fence Me In"?

A: Neither! Horses can't sing.

* * *

Q: Why does an elephant wear sunglasses?

A: If you were the one they were telling all these jokes about, you would want to hide too!

* * *

Q: I came to town and met three people. They were neither men, nor women, nor children. What were they?

A: A man, a woman, and a child.

* * *

Q: How do batteries get sick?

A: They get acid indigestion.

* * *

Q: Where does the Lone Ranger take his garbage?

A: To the dump, to the dump, to the dump, dump, dump.

Q: What do you call it when your teacher phones your parents to tell them you're doing poorly in school?

A: A bad connection.

* * *

Q: What kind of bird do you find in your mouth?

A: A swallow.

* * *

Q: What is a monster's normal eyesight?

A: 20/20/20/20/20.

* * *

Q: Who is Ferris?

A: He is a big wheel at the amusement park.

* * *

Q: What can you make that you can't see?

A: Noise.

* * *

Q: What kind of clothing lasts the longest?

A: Underwear, because it is never worn out.

* * *

Q: What animal has the highest level of intelligence?

A: The giraffe.

* * *

Q: What makes everyone sick except those who swallow it?

A: Flattery.

* * *

Q: What kind of fish do dogs like to chase?

A: Catfish

* * *

Q: What is it that you can't hold for five minutes yet it's as light as a feather?

A: Your breath.

* * *

Q: What is big and green and eats rocks.

A: A big green rock-eater.

* * *

Q: What headlines do women like least?

A: Wrinkles.

Q: How do you know when there's an elephant in your bed?

A: By the E on his pajamas.

* * *

Q: What's the best way to paint a rabbit?

A: With hare spray.

* * *

Q: What animal doesn't play fair?

A: The cheetah.

* * *

Q: What should you do to stop from getting sick the night before a trip?

A: Leave a day earlier.

* * *

Q: How do you keep an elephant from going through the eye of a needle?

A: Tie a knot in his tail.

* * *

Q: What goes ha-ha-ha-plop?

A: Someone who laughs his head off.

Q: What kind of clothes do Supreme Court judges wear?

A: Lawsuits.

* * *

Q: What is black and white and red all over?

A: A sunburned penguin.

* * *

Q: Do you know why the cow jumped over the moon?

A: The farmer had cold hands.

* * *

Q: What is it that even the smartest person will always overlook?

A: His nose.

* * *

Q: Which burns longer—a white candle or a black candle?

A: Neither. Both burn shorter.

* * *

Q: What has four legs and flies?

A: A pig.

Q: What remedy is there for someone who splits his sides with laughter?

A: Have him run as fast as he can—till he gets a stitch in his side.

* * *

Q: What's the biggest laundry problem giraffes have?

A: Ring around the collar.

* * *

Q: What is the best way to keep a skunk from smelling?

A: Hold his nose.

* * *

Q: Where does a sheep get his hair cut?

A: At the baa-baa shop.

* * *

Q: How much does an idiot weigh?

A: Step on the scales and see.

* * *

Q: What do you call a crate full of ducks?

A: A box of quackers.

Q: What two things can you never eat for breakfast?

A: Lunch and dinner.

* * *

Q: Why is a sleeping baby like a hijacking?

A: Because it's a kid napping.

* * *

Q: What two numbers multiplied together make 13?

A: One and 13.

* * *

Q: If an apple a day keeps the doctor away, what does an onion do?

A: It keeps EVERYBODY away.

* * *

Q: If all the money in the world were divided equally among the people, how much would each person get?

A: An equal amount.

* * *

Q: If the man you work for weighs 2000 pounds, what do you call him?

A: Boston. (Boss ton)

Q: What is it that floats on the water as light as a feather, yet a thousand men can't lift it?

A: A bubble.

* * *

Q: Where does a two-ton gorilla sit when he goes to the movies?

A: Anywhere he wants to!

* * *

Q: What do they call a man who gets paid for pinching people in the wrong places?

A: A policeman.

* * *

Q: What do Alexander the Great and Smokey the Bear have in common?

A: They both have the same middle name.

* * *

Q: Where does one see the handwriting on the wall?

A: In a phone booth or a rest room.

* * *

Q: What is found in the center of America and Australia?

A: The letter R.

Q: What do they call a fellow who introduces his best girl to his best friend?

A: An idiot.

* * *

Q: What kind of jokes does a scholar make?

A: Wisecracks.

* * *

Q: What do they call a dollar with all the taxes taken out?

A: A nickel.

* * *

Q: Why did Uncle Oscar name both of his sons Ed?

A: Because he had heard that two Eds are better than one.

* * *

Q: Who was the first man to make a monkey of himself?

A: Darwin.

* * *

Q: What do you call a frightened skin diver?

A: Chicken of the sea.

Q: What is the definition of a Chinese harbor?

A: A junkyard.

*   *   *

Q: Who killed a fourth of all the people in the world?

A: Cain, when he killed Abel.

*   *   *

Q: Which animal keeps the best time?

A: A watchdog.

*   *   *

Q: What's the best thing to do if you're going to be beheaded?

A: Stay calm and try not to lose your head.

*   *   *

Q: What is it called when a man marries the boss' daughter?

A: Fire insurance.

*   *   *

Q: Why do giraffes find it difficult to apologize?

A: It takes them a long time to swallow their pride.

Q: When does a farmer have the best chance to see his pigs?

A: When he has a sty on his eye.

* * *

Q: What's wrong with overeating?

A: It makes you thick to your stomach.

* * *

Q: What grows larger the more you take away?

A: A hole.

* * *

Q: What happens when the human body is completely submerged in water?

A: The telephone rings.

* * *

Q: Which bird can lift the heaviest weight?

A: The crane.

* * *

Q: What do hippopotamuses have that no other animals have?

A: Baby hippopotamuses.

Q: What goes putt-putt-putt-putt?
A: An over-par golfer.

* * *

Q: If a king sits on gold, who sits on Silver?
A: The Lone Ranger.

* * *

Q: What did the man do when he heard he was going to die?
A: He went into the living room.

* * *

Q: What color is a hiccup?
A: Burple.

* * *

Q: What is the longest sentence in the world?
A: "Go to prison for life."

* * *

Q: What is the last thing you take off before going to bed?
A: Your feet from the floor.

Q: What did the mayonnaise say to the refrigerator?

A: "Shut the door, I'm dressing."

* * *

Q: There is a donkey on one side of a deep river, and a bundle of hay on the other side. How can the donkey get the hay? There is no bridge, and he cannot swim. Do you give up?

A: So did the other donkey.

* * *

Q: What is full of holes and yet holds water?

A: A sponge.

* * *

Q: What is another name for a smart duck?

A: A wise quacker.

* * *

Q: Why did the chicken cross the road?

A: For fowl reasons.

* * *

Q: What has foot at each end and a foot in the middle?

A: A yardstick.

Q: What is the center of gravity?
A: V.

* * *

Q: What is the best thing about tiny TV sets?
A: Tiny commercials.

* * *

Q: What did the Gingerbread Boy find on his bed?
A: A cookie sheet, of course!

* * *

Q: Who was the world's greatest glutton?
A: A man who bolted a door, then threw up a window, and sat down and swallowed a whole story.

* * *

Q: To what question must you positively answer "Yes"?
A: What does Y-E-S spell.

* * *

Q: If you were dying and you had only a dime, what would you buy?
A: A pack of lifesavers.

Q: What happened to the duck that flew upside down?

A: It quacked up.

* * *

Q: What kind of song do you sing in a car?

A: A cartoon.

* * *

Q: If you were locked in a cemetery at night, how would you get out?

A: Use a skeleton key.

* * *

Q: What did Paul Revere say when he finished his famous ride?

A: Whoa!

* * *

Q: What is worse than raining cats and dogs?

A: Hailing taxis and buses.

* * *

Q: Why did the comedian's wife sue for divorce?

A: She claimed he was trying to joke her to death.

Q: What makes more noise than a cat howling at midnight?

A: Two cats howling at midnight.

* * *

Q: How does a musician clean a dirty tuba?

A: With a tuba toothpaste, naturally!

* * *

Q: What is the difference between an engineer and a teacher?

A: One minds the train, while the other trains the mind.

* * *

Q: What is worse than a centipede with corns?

A: A hippopotamus with chapped lips.

* * *

Q: What does everybody give and few take?

A: Advice.

* * *

Q: What happens to illegally parked frogs?

A: They get toad away.

Q: Why is an empty purse always the same?

A: Because there is never any change in it.

* * *

Q: Why was it that after Mrs. Jones had given her neighbor a butter churn, her neighbor gave her one back?

A: One good churn deserves another.

* * *

Q: Why is it hard to talk with a goat around?

A: Because he always butts in.

* * *

Q: What do you get when a bird flies into a fan?

A: Shredded tweet.

* * *

Q: Why does a hen lay an egg?

A: Because she can't lay a brick.

* * *

Q: What is deaf, dumb, and blind and always tells the truth?

A: A mirror.

Q: Why did the little boy go to sleep with birdseed in his shoes?

A: He wanted to feed his pigeon toes.

*   *   *

Q: What do you call a dumb skeleton?

A: A bone head.

*   *   *

Q: What is the surest way to double your money?

A: Fold it.

*   *   *

Q: What is smaller than an ant's mouth?

A: An ant's dinner.

*   *   *

Q: What age do most girls wish to attain?

A: Marriage.

*   *   *

Q: How do you remove varnish?

A: Take out the "r" and make it vanish.

Q: Why do we dress little girl babies in pink, and boy babies in blue?

A: Because they can't dress themselves.

* * *

Q: Why did the farmer put the cow on the scale?

A: He wanted to see how much the milky weighed.

* * *

Q: Why does a person who is sick lose his sense of touch?

A: Because he doesn't feel well.

* * *

Q: Which eat more grass—black sheep or white?

A: White, because there are more of them.

* * *

Q: Who wears a crown, lives in a delicatessen, and calls for his fiddlers three?

A: Old King Coleslaw.

* * *

Q: What is the best thing to put into cake?

A: Your teeth.

Q: What do you call a midget novelist?
A: A short story writer.

* * *

Q: What adds color and flavor to a very popular old pastime?
A: Lipstick.

* * *

Q: What is another name for a maternity dress?
A: A space suit.

* * *

Q: What do they call someone with a burning desire?
A: An arsonist.

* * *

Q: What is it that has never killed anybody, but seems to scare some people half to death?
A: Work.

* * *

Q: Who always goes to sleep first?
A: The loudest snorer.

Q: What is another name men give to their mistakes?

A: Experience.

* * *

Q: What is the name of the saddest bird alive?

A: The bluebird.

* * *

Q: What kind of doctor would a duck make?

A: A quack doctor.

* * *

Q: What is the best way to grow fat?

A: Raise pigs.

* * *

Q: Why can't the world ever come to an end?

A: Because it's round.

* * *

Q: What's the difference between kissing your sister and kissing your sweetheart?

A: About 25 seconds.

Q: What is smaller than an ant's mouth?
A: His teeth.

* * *

Q: What is the biggest handicap in golf?
A: Honesty.

* * *

Q: What is a witch's favorite plant?
A: Poison ivy.

* * *

Q: What do you get when you pour hot water down a rabbit hole?
A: A hot, cross bunny!

* * *

Q: What do they call the device that keeps flies in the house?
A: A window screen.

* * *

Q: Why can't it rain for two days continually?
A: Because there is always a night in between.

Q: What do you call a lady letter carrier?

A: A mail female.

* * *

Q: What two flowers grow best in a zoo?

A: Dandelion and the tiger lily.

* * *

Q: What weighs three tons, flies, and pulls Santa's sleigh?

A: Rudolph the Red-Nosed Rhinoceros.

* * *

Q: How do you stop a charging lion?

A: Take away his credit cards.

* * *

Q: Where do cows go when they want a night out?

A: To the mooovies!

* * *

Q: What is a diploma?

A: Da man who fixa da pipes when dey leak.

Q: What do you call a trainer who sticks his right hand in a lion's mouth?

A: Lefty.

*   *   *

Q: What is the difference between a rooster, Uncle Sam, and an old maid?

A: The rooster says, "Cock-a-doodle-doo"; Uncle Sam says, "Yankee-doodle-doo"; and an old maid says, "Any dude'll do."

*   *   *

Q: If you threw a green shoe into the Red Sea, what would it become?

A: Wet.

*   *   *

Q: Why should you borrow money from a pessimist?

A: Because he never expects to get it back.

*   *   *

Q: Why is a bank robbery like a pair of suspenders?

A: Because they are both holdups.

Q: What do they call a towel that you look at but never use?

A: A guest towel.

*   *   *

Q: How many hamburgers can you eat on an empty stomach?

A: Only one, because after that your stomach is no longer empty.

*   *   *

Q: What is the name for an older person who keeps your mother from spanking you?

A: A grandparent.

*   *   *

Q: Which state produces the most marriages?

A: A state of matrimony.

*   *   *

Q: What is the unpardonable sin against one's fellowman?

A: To be successful.

*   *   *

Q: How many peas in a pint?

A: One.

Q: What animal drops from the clouds?

A: The rain, dear.

* * *

Q: What kinds of animals can jump higher than the Statue of Liberty?

A: Any kind. The Statue of Liberty can't jump.

* * *

Q: What is the best way to make time go by fast?

A: Use the spur of the moment.

* * *

Q: What does 36 inches make in Glasgow?

A: One Scotland Yard.

* * *

Q: When does a boat show affection?

A: When it hugs the shore.

* * *

Q: What is the difference between a tuna fish and a piano?

A: You can't tune a fish.

Q: Do chickens jog?
A: No, but turkeys trot.

* * *

Q: How does one dinosaur tell another one to hurry up?
A: Pronto, Saurus!

* * *

Q: What fish is very evil?
A: The devilfish.

* * *

Q: How do you communicate with a fish?
A: Drop it a line.

* * *

Q: What is a cannibal?
A: Someone who is fed up with people.

* * *

Q: Where does a bird go when it's ill?
A: It goes for tweetment.

Q: Where do moths dance?
A: At a mothball.

*   *   *

Q: Why didn't the baby get hurt when he fell down?
A: Because he was wearing safety pins.

*   *   *

Q: How do you get down from an elephant?
A: You don't. You get down from a duck.

*   *   *

Q: When does ten plus seven equal thirteen?
A: When you add wrong.

*   *   *

Q: What nut sounds like a sneeze?
A: Cashew nut.

*   *   *

Q: Why is it hard to drive a golf ball?
A: Because it doesn't have a steering wheel.

Q: What do you call Batman and Robin when they get run over by a steamroller?

A: Flatman and Ribbon.

* * *

Q: What sits up with a woman when her husband is out late?

A: Her imagination.

* * *

Q: What colors would you paint the sun and the wind?

A: The sun rose and the wind blue.

* * *

Q: Why do single girls like the moon?

A: Because there's a man in it.

* * *

Q: What vegetable do you find in crowded streetcars and buses?

A: Squash.

* * *

Q: When a librarian goes fishing, what does she use for bait?

A: Bookworms.

Q: What can you hold without touching it?
A: Your breath.

* * *

Q: What is the best way to kill time?
A: Work it to death.

* * *

Q: When was beef the highest it has ever been?
A: When the cow jumped over the moon.

* * *

Q: How do you play Russian roulette in India?
A: You play the flute with six cobras around you—
and one of them is deaf.

* * *

Q: How intelligent is your pet duck?
A: Very intelligent! I'll prove it by having him
make a few wisequacks.

* * *

Q: What is black and white and black and white?
A: A penguin tumbling down an iceberg.

Q: What do you call the secret instructions for opening a zipper?

A: Zip code.

* * *

Q: What do you call a 30-pound book when you use it as a weapon?

A: Book club.

* * *

Q: What time is it when an elephant sits on your fence?

A: Time to buy a new fence.

* * *

Q: How can you tell there's an elephant under your bed?

A: The ceiling is very close.

* * *

Q: How can you tell if a student is hungry?

A: When he devours books.

* * *

Q: When a funny dairy farmer milks his cows, what do you call his jokes?

A: Udder nonsense!

Q: What is the difference between a shoe that hurts your foot and an oak tree?

A: One makes corns ache, the other makes acorns.

*   *   *

Q: What do you call a prankster who eats chili peppers for dinner?

A: A hot time in the old clown tonight.

*   *   *

Q: What is the best thing to do for that run-down feeling?

A: Get the license number of the car.

*   *   *

Q: What happened when two geese had a head-on collision?

A: They got goose bumps.

*   *   *

Q: Is Ballpoint really the name of your pig?

A: No—that's just his pen name.

*   *   *

Q: Who was King Midas?

A: He was the Greek king who fixed chariot mufflers.

Q: Why couldn't the pony talk.
A: He was a little horse.

* * *

Q: What is purple and 5000 miles long?
A: The Grape Wall of China.

* * *

Q: Why is E the most unfortunate of all the letters?
A: Because it is never in cash, always in debt, and never out of danger.

* * *

Q: Why is a pig in your kitchen like a house on fire?
A: The sooner it's put out the better.

* * *

Q: Who is the oldest whistler in the world?
A: The wind.

* * *

Q: Who was the greatest Irish inventor?
A: Pat. Pending.

Q: What makes more noise than a pig in a sty?
A: Two pigs.

* * *

Q: What did Mother Ghost say to Baby Ghost when
they got in the car?
A: Fasten your sheet belt.

* * *

Q: What's the best way to find out what a woman
thinks of you?
A: Marry her.

* * *

Q: Why do hummingbirds hum?
A: Because they can't remember the words.

* * *

Q: When does a girl admire a bachelor's voice?
A: When there is a ring in it.

* * *

Q: Who is Mexico's most famous fat man?
A: Pauncho Villa.

Q: What does a garden say when it laughs?
A: Hoe, hoe, hoe.

*　　*　　*

Q: What has no feet but always wears shoes?
A: The sidewalk.

*　　*　　*

Q: If you reached into your pants pockets and pulled out a ten-dollar bill from each, what would you have?
A: Somebody else's pants on.

*　　*　　*

Q: What does the envelope say when you lick it?
A: It just shuts up and says nothing.

*　　*　　*

Q: What's red, has tusks, and hates to be touched?
A: An elephant with a sunburn.

*　　*　　*

Q: Why did the three little pigs decide to leave home?
A: They thought their father was an awful boar.

More
Harvest House Books
by Bob Phillips

THE ALL AMERICAN JOKE BOOK

A riotous, fun-filled collection of over 800 anecdotes, puns, and jokes.

BIBLE FUN

Jam-packed full of brain-teasing crossword puzzles,
intricate mazes, word jumbles, and other mind
benders. *Bible Fun* will keep you occupied for
hours—with the added bonus of honing your Bible
knowledge. Sharpen your pencil and put your
thinking cap on—you're about to be a-maze-d!

THE LAST OF THE GOOD CLEAN JOKES

The master joker edits and arranges wisecracks, rib
ticklers, and zany puns.

MORE GOOD CLEAN JOKES

An entertaining fun-book designed for public
speakers, pastors, and everyone who enjoys good
clean jokes.

THE RETURN OF THE GOOD CLEAN JOKES

Over 900 quips, anecdotes, gags, puns, and
wisecracks.

Other Good Harvest House Books

PROVERBS FOR PEOPLE
by Vern McClellan

Clever, provocative proverbs are matched with a corresponding Bible reference and illustration that will bring a smile and a cause for reflection with the turn of each page. Here's a sample: Proverb: He who gossips usually winds up in his own mouthtrap. Proverbs 16:28: An evil man sows strife; gossip separates the best of friends.

QUIPS, QUOTES, AND QUESTS
by Vern McClellan

You'll never be without a wise or witty saying after you read *Quips, Quotes, and Quests*. This inspiring collection of 1,098 famous (and infamous) quotations, Bible verses, and common sense sayings is a handy reference book for the whole family. If you like stimulating, insightful one-liners, this is the book for you.

PROVERBS, PROMISES, AND PRINCIPLES
by Vern McClellan

This inspiring book is jammed with penetrating insights and poignant points that will add exciting new dimensions to your life and conversation. If you're a teacher, preacher, writer, researcher, parent or student, you'll find humorous, practical proverbs, timely Bible promises, and powerful principles to apply to living.